972

Exploring the Aztec Empire

Aztec warriors with their prisoners.

3000 BC	2000 BC	1000 BC

Ancient Egyptians (3000–332 BC)

Ancient Gr

Part of an Aztec drawing showing the headdresses, animal skins and other decorations that went with different positions in Aztec society.

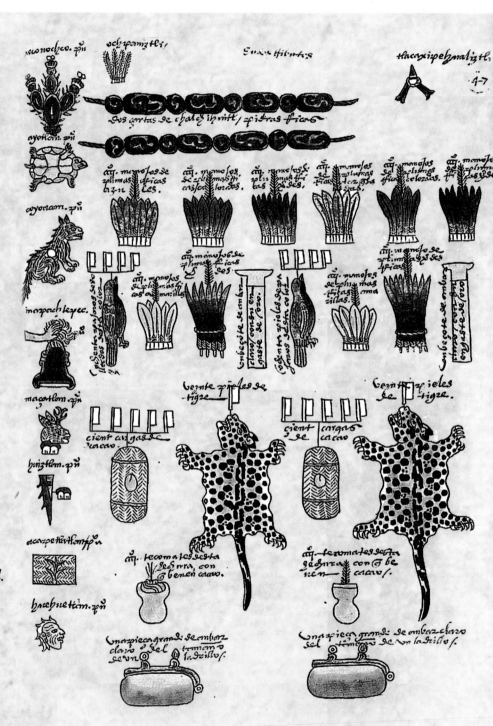

Note: Some of the names may look alike.

Teotihuacan, the very ancient capital with the Pyramid of the Sun is pronounced *te–ohti–wacan.*

Tenochtitlan, the capital of the Aztecs is pronounced *ten–oach–tich–lan.*

The Aztec god Huitzilopochtli is pronounced *wee–tsee–loh–poch–tlee.*

The end of many words is *–catl.* This means 'people'.

Aztecs timeline

Aztecs left homeland in search of new home.

Aztecs settled near Lake Texcoco.

1100	1200	1300

Aztecs arrived in Valley of Mexico.

Tenochtitlan was founded. First temple built by Aztecs.

Aztecs (1100–1521)

0   1000 AD   2000 AD

–146BC)

Anglo-Saxons (450–1066)

Tudors (1485–1603)

Victorians (1837–1901)

Romans (700BC–476AD)

Vikings (800–1066/1400)

Contents

Meet the Aztecs 4

How do we know about the Aztecs? 6

Ancestors 8

The arrival of the Aztecs 10

Aztec gods 12

The Aztec calendar 14

The city of Tenochtitlan 16

The Temple of Tenochtitlan 18

Aztec army 20

Trade and markets 22

Getting enough food 24

At home and at school 26

The Spaniards 28

The end of Aztec times 30

Glossary and Index 32

Look up the **bold** words in the glossary
on page 32 of this book.

Acamapichtli becomes
first ruler of Aztecs.

Tepanecs defeated.
Aztecs rule whole valley.

Mochtezuma I
died.

Mochtezuma II becomes ruler. Aztec
empire at height of its powers.

1400   1500   1600

Tenoch, Aztec Priest-Ruler, died.
Aztecs ruled by Tepanecs.

Mochtezuma I
started rule.

Tenochtitlan destroyed
by flood. 1452-4 Famine.

Tenochtitlan destroyed.
Cortes comes to Mexico.
Mochtezuma II killed.

- The priests were frightening to look at! They painted their skins and were often covered in wounds where they had beaten themselves. They probably wore dark cloaks, sewn with skulls, and tall headdresses of feathers. Their hair was long – a priest could not cut or comb his hair – and was stiff with the blood from many **sacrifices**.

Meet the Aztecs

The Aztecs were one of the great North American **civilisations**. Today the most powerful people in North America live in the United States, but this is a quite recent change.

Before the arrival of Europeans, the most powerful civilisations lived in what is now Mexico.

The Aztecs had a highly ordered society, ruled over by a king. There were also priests and nobles, labourers and slaves.

They influenced both North and Central America by their trade and **conquests**.

The land that the Aztecs came to rule was powerful and rich. Many people lived there. At the time of the Aztecs there were more people living in their great city called

Teotihuacan (near modern Mexico City) than in any city in Europe.

The Aztecs rose to power over many centuries but their civilisation crumbled away in just a few short months. This is a unique story that you will read about in this book. First, let us meet the Aztecs.

Q **Where did the Aztecs live?**

How do we know about the Aztecs?

Today there is almost nothing left from Aztec times. So, how do we know about them? The answer is that the Aztecs had **scribes** who kept records and made paintings showing their way of life. Little bits and pieces of them still survive and some are shown on this page. The Aztecs were conquered by the Spanish. The Spanish also wrote about the life of the Aztecs and made paintings of them.

This painting names the cities the Aztecs conquered. To show they were conquered, the Aztecs drew the temples toppled over on their pyramids.

Did you know… ?

• The Aztecs did not use letters to write. Instead they used small pictures called **glyphs**. This is similar to the ancient Egyptian hieroglyphs. The glyphs were used to remind the priests and other people of the stories that they had learned from their elders by word of mouth. (The writing you see here was added later by Spaniards.)

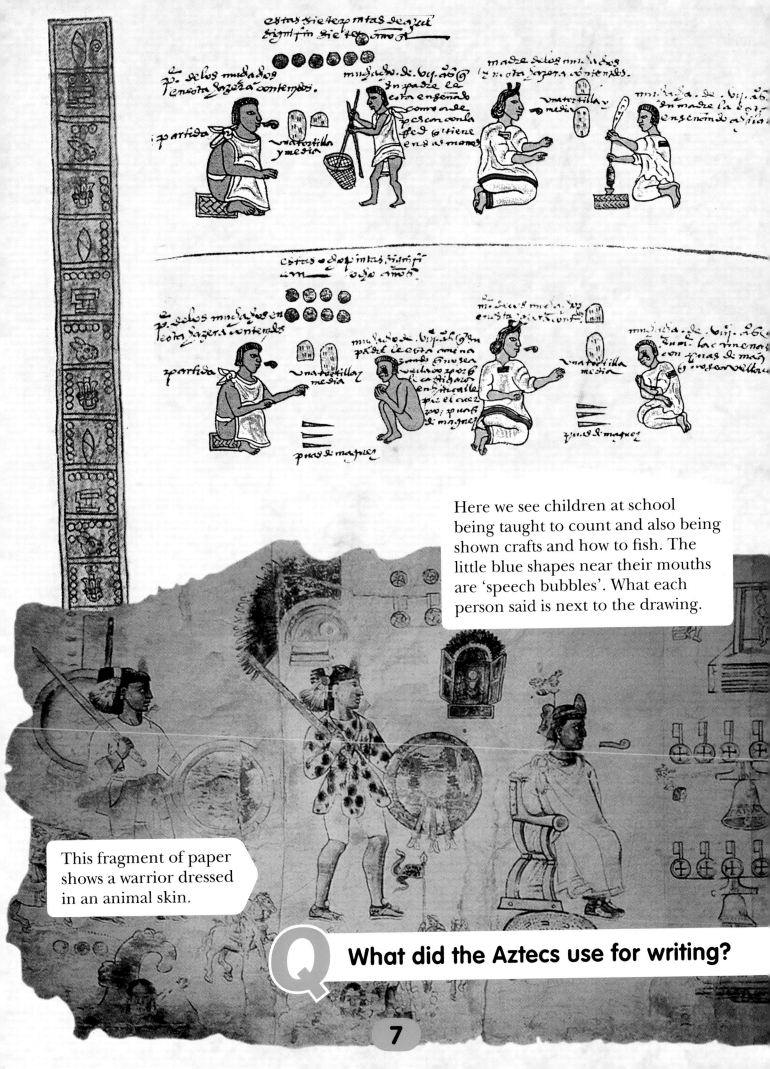

Here we see children at school being taught to count and also being shown crafts and how to fish. The little blue shapes near their mouths are 'speech bubbles'. What each person said is next to the drawing.

This fragment of paper shows a warrior dressed in an animal skin.

Q What did the Aztecs use for writing?

This was called the Pyramid of the Sun by the Aztecs. It is nearly 75 m tall.

Each of these pyramids once had a temple on top.

Ancestors

The Aztecs came to power in a land rich in history. Many powerful civilisations had come and gone before them. Three thousand years ago, central America was home to the powerful **Olmec** people. Their civilisation lasted until about 400 BC. Although their power over others faded away, their way of life carried on, and their successors built the amazing city of Teotihuacan in the Valley of Mexico. It covered an area of over 82 square kilometres and was a place of giant pyramids connected by a central road 3 km long, called the 'Avenue of the Dead'.

The city may have been home to 150,000 people. Around the central temples and palaces there were marketplaces, schools and homes. The walls were plastered over with lime and painted in splendid colours. The city also had paved roads and underground water pipes.

This is the Avenue of the Dead.

Q What was this place like when the Aztecs arrived?

The Teotihuacan empire lasted for nearly 1,000 years and then it suddenly vanished, just as the Olmec one had done before it.

Although all of these people had vanished by the time of the Aztecs, they were to be very important in the lives of the Aztecs who followed them.

Did you know… ?

- The Pyramid of the Sun rises in five giant steps.
- It was built over a sacred cave.
- On the top was a temple.
- When the Aztecs arrived, Teotihuacan was a ruin. The Aztecs thought of it as a place where men were made into gods.
- It was the Aztecs who gave it, and its pyramids, the names we use today. Its original name is unknown.

The arrival of the Aztecs

Some time after the builders of Teotihuacan the **Toltecs** rose to power.

During their reign the Toltecs quarrelled among themselves and one group was forced from the area. Their priests **prophesied** that one day they would return on a day named 'One Reed' along with their god who would have a white face. This prophesy was to be very important to the history of all North America (see page 28).

Sometime later the Toltecs were overrun by enemies and the remaining cities struggled for power. To get power, each city hired extra soldiers. Some of the soldiers they hired belonged to a tribe of ruffians called the Mexicas. The country of Mexico is now named after them. These people would later call themselves Aztecs.

Over time, the Aztecs arranged marriages between their people and neighbouring city leaders who were descended from the Olmecs and Toltecs.

In this way, by 1472 the small tribe of ruffians had made themselves into the most powerful people in the Valley of Mexico.

Then the Aztecs changed their history. They rewrote it to say they were descended from the ancient Olmecs and Toltecs.

A ceremonial Aztec mask.

Did you know… ?

- The Aztecs were first called the Mexicas. The name may come from the word *Mexitli* (the weed that grows in Lake Texcoco), because at the time the Mexicas originally arrived in the Mexico Basin, the only place they were allowed to settle was on an island in the lake. They were not allowed to catch fish, and to avoid starvation they had to eat the weed. So the name Mexica could mean "weed people".

Q **What were the first Aztecs called?**

Aztec gods

The Aztecs worshipped many gods and goddesses. However, the Aztecs praised the Sun god, Huitzilopochtli, most of all, for he told the Aztecs where to build their city.

He was also the god of war and the god who, the Aztecs believed, had to be worshipped by offering human sacrifices.

Quetzalcoatl

(meaning 'Feathered snake')
He was the god of morning and the evening star and thus the symbol of death and rebirth. He was also the god of the wind. Quetzalcoatl was often shown with a beard. The temples to him were round because the wind could easily blow round them.

Huitzilopochtli

(meaning 'Hummingbird')
Huitzilopochtli was the last of the five Suns, and so was the Sun god. The Aztecs believed that dead warriors were born again as hummingbirds. Huitzilopochtli, in the form of a hummingbird, was carried on high in front of the Aztec army when they went into battle. Huitzilopochtli also took the form of an eagle.

It was Huitzilopochtli who instructed the Aztecs to found their city, Tenochtitlan, in the lake of the Valley of Mexico.

One spot was particularly sacred because it was here that priests saw an eagle sitting on a rock eating a snake. The site later became a place where a great temple was built.

Huitzilopochtli is shown as a warrior whose armour and helmet were made of humming bird feathers. His upper face was shown black, everything else was blue. The Aztecs believed that Huitzilopochtli needed feeding each day and that the Aztecs, the people of the Sun, had to provide him with hearts and blood.

Tezacatlipoca

(meaning 'Smoking mirror')
He had a black mirror made of black volcanic glass on his chest in which he saw all the thoughts and deeds of people. He was the god of the Great Bear pattern of stars in the night sky. He was thought of as a jaguar because jaguars have spotted coats like the night sky, and priests wore jaguar skins to represent him.

He was in charge of schools for young boys and saw that they got military training. He was also the god who protected slaves and stopped their masters ill-treating them, but he needed sacrifices to keep him happy. Every year, during the fifth month, the priests chose a young and handsome war prisoner. For one year he was given everything he desired and treated as the living god. At the end of this time a feast day was declared and he was killed as the sacrifice.

Chalchiuhtlicue

The Aztecs believed that in the history of the world there had been four Suns before the one we now see. The fourth Sun was Chalchiuhtlicue, the water goddess.

Tlaloc

(meaning 'The one who makes thing sprout')
He was the rain god. Tlaloc was shown as a man wearing clouds, a crown of heron feathers, sandals and carrying rattles to make thunder. He lived with the goddess of freshwater lakes and streams.

Tlaloc was greatly feared because he could cause floods and droughts. It was he who set hurricanes and thunderbolts on the people.

Q **Why did the Aztecs sacrifice people?**

The Aztec calendar

Many American peoples had calendars. The Aztecs had two calendars – a religious calendar and a **solar** calendar. The religious calendar was 260 days and the solar calendar was 365 days. These two calendars were combined to give a 52 year 'century'.

Remember that the Aztecs used **glyphs**, not writing. Days were made up of 20 glyphs, together with the numbers 1 to 13. Each day sign is dedicated to a god.

In the religious calendar each of the twenty 13-day periods, or weeks, is shown separately, together with the picture of the god connected to that 'week'.

House

Lizard

Serpent

Death

Deer

Rabbit

Did you know… ?

- In the Aztec history of the world there had been four creations (times of the Sun) before the one we have now. The fourth creation was caused by Chalchiuhtlicue, who was also the water goddess.

There is a calendar carved on this sunstone, but it was used as a sacrificial altar. The purpose of calendars was to tell the Aztecs when to perform rituals to their gods. Without this the Aztecs believed the world would come to an end.

This sunstone was carved and dedicated to the main Aztec god: the Sun. It weighs almost 25 tons, has a diameter of just under 4 m, and a thickness of 1 m.

Crocodile

Flower

Rain

Wind

Flint knife

Movement

2nd Sun: Wind

1st Sun: Jaguar

Vulture

3rd Sun: Rain

4th Sun: Water

Eagle

Jaguar

Reed

Grass

Dog

Monkey

Q **How did the Aztecs name their 'weeks'?**

The city of Tenochtitlan

The capital city of the Aztec empire was Tenochtitlan, now the site of modern-day Mexico City. It was home to 200,000 people and built on some small islands in Lake Texcoco.

The city was divided into 60 districts where the different **clans** lived. Each clan had its own temple complex and its own farming gardens – called **chinampas**.

Houses were made of wood and mud. Roofs were made of reed thatch. Only pyramids, temples and palaces were made of stone. Canals were used as the main way of getting about.

Tenochtitlan had 25 pyramids, each with a temple on top. Every temple was dedicated to a different god or a hero of the past. The temples were surrounded by plazas and gardens.

The city was run according to class. A boy growing up as the son of a nobleman would have become a government official, a teacher or a scribe. But when he grew up he would also have to do military service and then he was expected to lead his troops into battle.

If he grew up as an ordinary worker, he would be trained as a farmer, a labourer, a fisherman or a stonemason whose job it was to build and repair the temples. He might also be a soldier or a merchant. But he could not change class.

Did you know… ?

- Each day the streets were cleaned and the refuse was collected and carried away on barges.
- The nobles lived in two-storey houses with gardens in which roses and other flowers were grown.
- There were **aviaries** for rare birds, including those from whom the feathers would be made into **headdresses**.
- Nobody was allowed to drink alcohol until they were 70 years old!

The Temple of Tenochtitlan

Blue bands represent rain

The Great Temple of Tenochtitlan was in the centre of the city. It was made of two stepped pyramids rising side by side 60m above the city. These pyramids were like two sacred mountains; the blue and white temple on the left was Tonacatepetl, the Hill of Sustenance. This temple was for Tlaloc, the god of rain. The red and white temple on the right was the Hill of Coatepec, birthplace of the Aztec war god Huitzilopochtli. Inside each temple there was an image of the god. Pairs of large serpent heads were placed at the feet of the pyramids. Near the top sculptures of figures held flagpoles with flags of bright paper and feathers.

In front of each temple was a huge stone – the sacrifice stone.

Did you know… ?

- The main temple area had 25 pyramids, 5 speaking halls, 7 frames on which the skulls of the sacrificed were displayed, and 2 ball game fields.
- Because the Aztecs feared their gods they believed that only human sacrifices would make the gods be kind to them.
- They mostly sacrificed captured warriors.

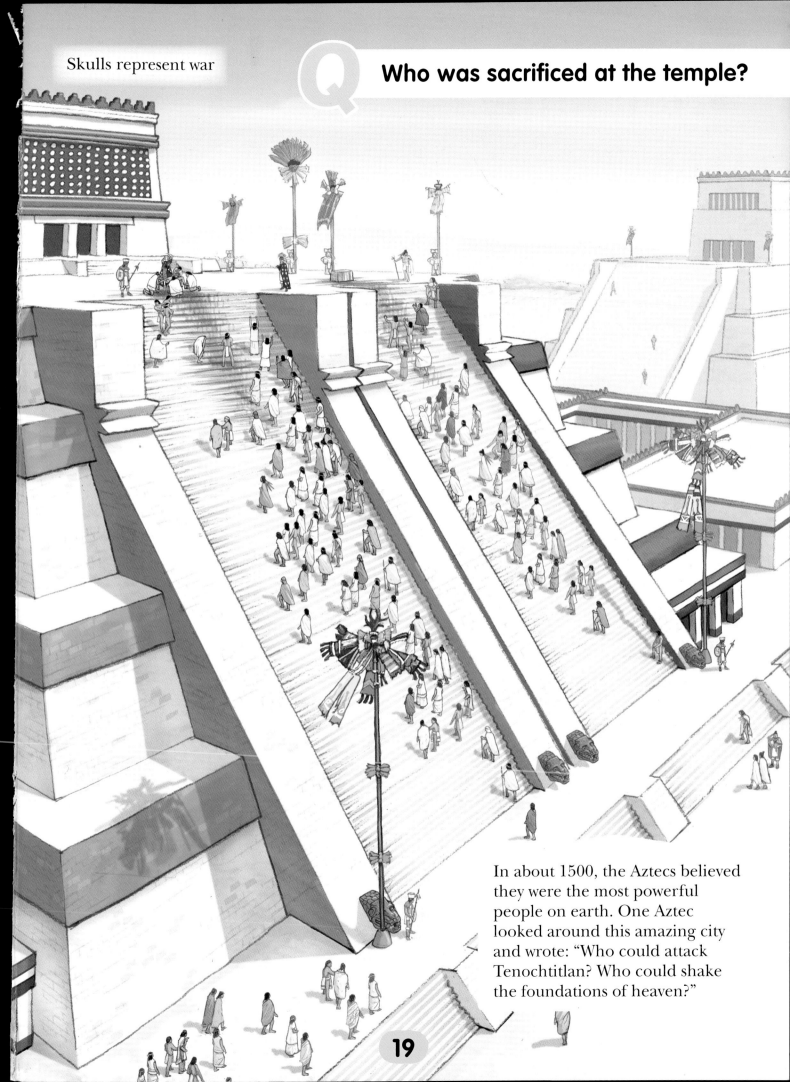

Skulls represent war

Who was sacrificed at the temple?

In about 1500, the Aztecs believed they were the most powerful people on earth. One Aztec looked around this amazing city and wrote: "Who could attack Tenochtitlan? Who could shake the foundations of heaven?"

Aztec army

The Aztecs had one of the most powerful armies in the world. It had over 200,000 men.

It was organised just like a modern army, with generals and lower ranks.

The generals were always nobles. Some were priests as well.

The warriors carried shields and had feather headdresses. The feathers were used so that the commander could see his troops on the battlefield. Some warriors also dressed in the skins of wild animals, such as the jaguar.

The Aztecs were a Bronze Age people, that is their strongest metal was bronze. They had not discovered iron. So they preferred to use Stone Age weapons: wooden spears with slivers of sharp flint set into them. These flints were as sharp as any steel blade.

The Aztec warriors must have been very fearsome to look at, with their tall headdresses. They also had spears with sharp blades of stone set into them. These were for slashing, not stabbing. It would have been a very bloody battle with lots of people being wounded rather than killed outright.

Did you know… ?

- That the Aztecs thought that sacrificing defeated warriors to their gods was not very different from the European way of waging war: Europeans killed the warriors during the battle; Aztecs killed the warriors after the battle.

In this closeup you can see an Aztec sacrificial dagger – made from a pointed piece of stone with a wooden handle.

Q Why did the warriors wear bright uniforms?

Trade and markets

The Aztecs traded with peoples far and wide. They also had goods brought to them from the cities they had conquered. It was a kind of **tax**.

Much of this wealth found its way to the markets, where people could get precious stones and cotton, flowers, rare birds and many other things.

So many goods were on offer that a market was held every day, with tens of thousands of people buying and selling. Farmers brought some of their produce, potters sold their wares, and so on. There were businessmen who traded goods with other parts of America. These people were organised into **guilds**, each guild trading in one product.

One of the many busy marketplaces.

Did you know… ?

- Several types of money were used. For cheap goods they used cacao beans. A small rabbit was worth 30 beans, and a turkey egg cost 3 beans.
- For buying more expensive items, rolls of cotton cloth were used for money. Twenty rolls of cotton was enough 'money' to support an ordinary worker for one year in Tenochtitlan.

Q **What could be bought in the marketplace?**

Getting enough food

The lands around Tenochtitlan were dry for much of the year and did not give good crops. So how did this enormous city feed itself?

They made **chinampas** – floating market gardens. They first wove sticks into mats. Then they used wooden spades to get mud from the lake bed and they laid this on the mat of sticks to make little islands. They grew crops in the chinampas mud and **irrigated** them with lake water.

Each clan had its own chinampas and if they had more than enough food to feed themselves they would sell the extra in the markets. In fact, they often had space to spare, and this allowed them to grow luxuries such as flowers, which women then sold in the markets.

The Aztecs fished in the lake and the canals using nets made of woven grass, and pointed wooden spears.

Did you know… ?

- The Aztecs were mostly vegetarians as meat was hard to find. They did keep turkeys.
- The main cereal was maize; the main vegetables were beans and squash; and the main spice was chillis.
- They used cactus-looking plants, called agaves, as a source of fibres for weaving ropes and clothing for poor people, and for sugar.

- Cacao beans were used to make a cold chocolate drink.
- They also ate insects because they are a very concentrated kind of protein.
- The Aztecs kept beehives and harvested honey.
- The chinampas could provide up to seven crops a year.
- The Aztecs had a much better diet before they were conquered by the Spaniards than afterwards.

Q How were chinampas made?

At home and at school

Until they were fourteen, children learned at home. They had to learn a collection of sayings, called the *sayings of the old*. This is how they passed on their history and myths.

At 15, all boys and girls went to school. The Aztecs were one of the first peoples in the world to have compulsory education for children. There were two types of schools for boys: one kind (a sort of technical school) taught practical and military skills, while the other kind (a sort of secondary school) taught writing, astronomy, statesmanship and religion.

Girls were taught how to look after a home and raise children, and about religion. They were not taught to read or write.

While at school all children were kept under strict conditions, teaching them to be tough and hardy people.

26

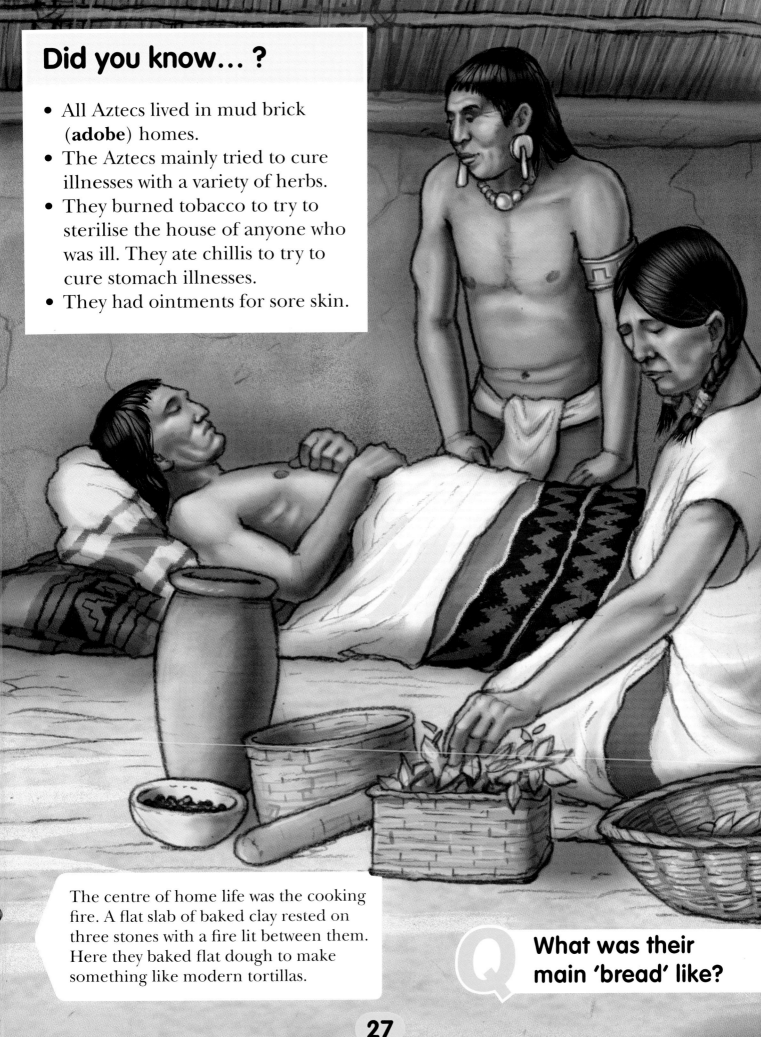

Did you know... ?

- All Aztecs lived in mud brick (**adobe**) homes.
- The Aztecs mainly tried to cure illnesses with a variety of herbs.
- They burned tobacco to try to sterilise the house of anyone who was ill. They ate chillis to try to cure stomach illnesses.
- They had ointments for sore skin.

The centre of home life was the cooking fire. A flat slab of baked clay rested on three stones with a fire lit between them. Here they baked flat dough to make something like modern tortillas.

Q What was their main 'bread' like?

The Spaniards

In the year called One Reed, the emperor, Mochtezuma II, was the most powerful person in the whole of North America and ruled over 10 million people. He was very superstitious and the priests showed him signs that disaster was coming.

For several years there had been bad signs: a burning light (a comet) had travelled across the sky, temples had been destroyed by lightning, a huge tongue of fire (a volcanic eruption) had poured out of a nearby mountain.

Then, one day, messengers arrived telling of houses floating on the sea (ships), of men (the Spaniard, Hernan Cortes and his troops) clothed in metal (armour) and, most important of all, they had white skin. It was just as it had been foretold. The god Quetzalcoatl had returned. Mochtezuma must please the god. He must send gifts.

When the messengers arrived, Cortes used a very clever tactic: he terrified the Aztec messengers who had brought gifts by firing a canon and blowing up a tree. They rushed back to tell Mochtezuma the amazing power of the god.

When Cortes reached Tenochtitlan, he was amazed by the wealth and organisation of the city. It was far more advanced than any city he had seen at home. Cortes wrote, "the people of this city are dressed with elegance and courtly bearing."

28

Did you know… ?

- Hernan Cortes was sent by Spain to try to get as much gold and silver as he could.
- The people Cortes first met were from nearby cities who were enemies of the Aztecs. Cortes made these enemies his allies.
- Cortes fell in love with one of the native women, who then went with him as an interpreter.
- Mochtezuma could have sent out his vast army and defeated Cortes, but he could not move because of his own prophesy that the god was returning.
- Spanish explorer troops were called **conquistadors**, conquering ones.

Q What did Cortes think of the Aztecs?

The end of Aztec times

Cortes was horrified by the Aztec religion because it needed human sacrifice. He had also been sent to get treasure for the King of Spain and the only way he would be able to do this was by treachery.

The Spaniards captured Mochtezuma and held him captive for six months while they tried to take all the wealth of the city.

Mochtezuma's brother then took over as emperor and formed an army. The Spaniards tried to escape but were slowed down by the weight of the treasure they were carrying, and many were killed.

When the Spaniards were gone the Aztecs wrote, "Once again the temples can be swept out, and the dirt (created by the way the Spaniards lived) removed."

Although Cortes had been driven out, he and his men had brought with them the plague, called smallpox, and other diseases. The Aztecs had no natural protection: the disease began to kill them in huge numbers.

With the city so weakened, Cortes and the Aztec enemies came back. The battle for the city lasted four months and the city was finally crushed.